Learner Services

Please return
on or before
the last date
stamped below

KT-418-744

Public   acy

Hodder Murray

A MEMB

213 478

Acknowledgements

Photo credits

pp. iv, 5, 7, 12, 21 © Colorsport; p. 17 © Mirrorpix; p. 27 © Dusan Vranic/AP/Empics

Every effort has been made to trace all copyright holders, but if any have been inadvertently overlooked the Publishers will be pleased to make the necessary arrangements at the first opportunity.

Orders: please contact Bookpoint Ltd, 130 Milton Park, Abingdon, Oxon OX14 4SB. Telephone: (44) 01235 827720. Fax: (44) 01235 400454. Lines are open 9.00–6.00, Monday to Saturday, with a 24-hour message answering service. Visit our website at www.hoddereducation.co.uk

© Peter Leigh 2006
First published in 2006 by
Hodder Murray, an imprint of Hodder Education,
a member of the Hodder Headline Group
338 Euston Road
London NW1 3BH

Impression number   10 9 8 7 6 5 4 3 2 1
Year   2010 2009 2008 2007 2006

Cover photo © Darren Walsh/Rex Features
Typeset in Palatino 14/20pt by Fakenham Photosetting Limited, Fakenham, Norfolk
Printed in Great Britain by CPI, Bath

A catalogue record for this title is available from the British Library
ISBN-10: 0 340 914 033
ISBN-13: 978 0340 914 038

Contents

You'll never walk alone at Liverpool.
FA Cup Final, 1989.

1 You'll Never Walk Alone

When you walk through the storm,
Hold your head up high,
And don't be afraid of the dark,
At the end of the storm,
Is a golden sky,
And the sweet silver song of the lark,
Walk on through the wind,
Walk on through the rain,
Though your dreams be tossed and blown.
Walk on, walk on,
With hope in your hearts,
And you'll never walk alone,
You'll never walk alone.

The song says it all!
It's Liverpool's song.

Everyone knows it,
and lots of clubs use it,
but it began in Liverpool
on the Kop at Anfield,
which is Liverpool's ground.

The words mean something special for Liverpool.
The song says Liverpool have walked
through the storm,
and seen the golden sky at the end.

They've seen the glory
and the tragedy,
the best
and the worst.

They have been
the most famous club in the world,
and the most hated!

2 Bill Shankly

The glory started in 1959,
when Bill Shankly became manager.
Under him
Liverpool won the League three times,
and the Cup twice.
And they won the UEFA Cup in Europe.

Bill Shankly is one of the
great names of football.
He was Scottish.
He was short and sharp,
and there were hundreds of stories about him.

His sayings became famous:

'I had no education,
so I had to use my brains.'

'We murdered them, Nil–Nil!'

Shankly's best jokes were about Everton,
the other team in Liverpool.

'There are two great teams in Liverpool.
Liverpool and Liverpool Reserves!'

'On my days off
I like to get right away from football.
I go and watch Everton!'

Everyone laughed when he said,
'Football isn't a matter of life or death,
it's more important than that!'

But later they remembered it with bitterness.

The team loved Bill Shankly,
and were a little bit afraid of him.

He got great players,
like Ian St John and Kevin Keegan,
and made them proud to play for Liverpool.

Kevin Keegan playing for Liverpool.

His way of playing was very simple.
'You just keep going –
you keep hold of the ball,
you knock it about,
you use your talents
and play to your strengths.
But you always keep hold of the ball!
You get a lot of movement
and away you go!
And you never, ever give up!'

This is the way Liverpool have played
ever since.
And it has worked.

Once, in the middle of a game,
one of the other team
came up to the Liverpool captain
and said,
'Can we have a go now, please?'

He hadn't touched the ball
for the whole game!

'There are two great teams in Liverpool.
Liverpool and Liverpool Reserves!'
Bill Shankly, Liverpool Manager, 1959–74.

This way of playing sounds very simple,
but it's difficult to do.
It needs players who will give their best.
It needs players who care
more about the team
than themselves.

Bill Shankly was so good
because he made the whole team like this.
Before he would sign a player
he would study him carefully.
Not just how he played,
but how he looked,
and how he behaved.
He wanted to see if the player
was right for Liverpool.

If a player wasn't trying his best,
Bill Shankly would make him suffer.
But if a player played well,
Bill would praise him.

One player said,
'When you pull on that red shirt,
and you run out at Anfield,
you feel ten feet tall!'

3 Bob Paisley

In 1974, Liverpool won the Cup.
It was a great game
and Liverpool deserved to win.
Liverpool were on top of the world.
They had won the league the year before,
and they had a young team
who could win anything.

And then Bill Shankly retired!

People could not believe it.
Liverpool were at their best.
Bill Shankly could not retire!

Everyone tried to get him
to change his mind.
But it was no good.
He never changed his mind
once it was made up.

One fan said,
'We have seen the best.
We've seen Liverpool since Shankly.
We have seen the cream,
and seen good, good, good football!'
The main gates at Anfield
were renamed The Shankly Gates,
in honour of the great man.

But who would be the new manager?
It would have to be someone good,
someone famous,
to follow the great Bill Shankly!

Then it was announced
that Bob Paisley was the new manager.
Everyone said, 'Who?'
Bob Paisley had been assistant to Bill Shankly.
Nobody had ever heard of him.
Everyone groaned.
It would never be the same at Liverpool!
They were on their way down.

Everyone was wrong!

Under Bob Paisley
Liverpool became
simply the best club in the world.
They won the league – six times!
And they won the League Cup
three times in a row!
All teams wanted to win the European Cup
(now called the Champions League)
and it was the best cup to win.
Liverpool won it three times!

They beat all the famous teams in Europe,
like Real Madrid and AC Milan.
They were the top team in Europe
and they stayed at the top.
Everyone was scared of Liverpool.

Their best defenders were
Emlyn Hughes and Alan Hansen.
They could change defence into attack in seconds.
When they gave up football,
they both appeared on television.

Liverpool's most famous player, Kenny Dalglish, 1979.

Graeme Souness was the playmaker.
He set the moves up
and made them happen.

When he finished playing,
he became a manager
and even managed Liverpool itself.

There was also Ian Rush and John Barnes,
who could do impossible things with the ball.
All these players became
Footballer of the Year.

But Liverpool's most famous player
was Kenny Dalglish.
He was named Footballer of the Year twice.
He was a striker
and never seemed to miss.
He was sharp and very fast.
Kenny seemed to know
what was happening behind him.
He scored more goals than anyone else!

In 1985, Kenny Dalglish became
manager of Liverpool!
Liverpool always surprises people
but this was the biggest surprise of the lot
because Kenny Dalglish was still playing!
For five years he was player/manager.
That had never happened before
at this level of football.

But with success can come disaster.
Love can turn to hate.
In 1985, Liverpool became the
darkest name in football,
the most hated club in Europe.

4 Dark Days: Heysel

In 1985, it was the final of the European Cup
between Liverpool
and the Italian club Juventus.
It was held at the Heysel Stadium in Belgium.
The stadium was not very good
and the planning was not very good.

But nothing can excuse what happened.

Just before the match,
a crowd of Liverpool fans
charged the Juventus fans.

Fights broke out all over the ground.
A wall collapsed
and people were crushed underneath.

But the fighting still carried on.
There were not enough police to stop it.

The start of the game was delayed.
Some Liverpool players came out
to calm the crowd down.
It was no good.

When the fighting had stopped,
it was found that 39 people had died.
They had been crushed to death.
They were all Italian.

One man said about the Liverpool fans,
'How can I forget those people?
I saw them with my own eyes,
violent, raging,
spitting at the dead and injured.'
He was the father of one of the dead.

The game went ahead after a delay,
but the players were too shocked
to play properly.

Many had been crying in the dressing room.
They never wanted to play football again.
What was the point of playing football
if it was going to end like this?

No excuse.
Heysel Stadium tragedy, 1985.

Bill Shankly's words came back
to haunt them.

'Football isn't a matter of life or death –
it's more important than that!'

Liverpool lost, but what did that matter?

Millions all over Europe
had watched it on TV.
They were horrified.
They blamed it all on Liverpool.

Fourteen Liverpool fans were put in prison,
and all English clubs
were banned from Europe.
It was six years before the ban was lifted.

Liverpool was the most hated name in Europe
and in England itself.
It was the worst day
in the history of Liverpool.

But more was still to come.

5 Dark Days: Hillsborough

In 1989, Liverpool was
in the semi-final of the FA Cup.
It was against Nottingham Forest
and was going to be played at Hillsborough.
All the Liverpool fans were at one end.
They all crowded in,
more and more of them,
all keen to see the match.

The crowd got tighter and tighter.
There were too many in the space.
Those at the front
were crushed against the railings.
Many of them were children.

The match started.
There were still people outside.
They pressed forward.
They didn't want to miss anything.
The crush got worse.
Police horses were lifted into the air.

Nobody realised how bad it was.
People started to die.
The game carried on.
The players didn't know what was happening.
Some fans got on to the pitch.
Alan Hansen told them to get off.
'There's people dying in there,' said one.
'Al, there's people dying in there!'

Bruce Grobbelaar was the goal keeper.
He went to take a goal kick.
He could hear voices behind him,
through the railings.
'They're killing us! Bruce, they're killing us!'
He forgot about the game.
He screamed at the police,
'Open the gates! Open the effing gates!'
But they were helpless.
The referee saw something was wrong
and stopped the game.

No comfort for Kenny Dalglish.
The worst disaster in the history of British football.
Hillsborough, 1989.

The players went back to the dressing room.
They thought it was just a delay.
Alan Hansen said,
'We were just waiting to go back on,
trying to keep ourselves ready.
Then the referee came in and said,
"There's not going to be a game.
There's big trouble.
We think people have died."
And then the news, 11 people,
then 22.
And we thought, it can't go any further.
There can't be any more.'

In the end there were 95 people dead
and 170 injured.
It was the worst disaster
in the history of British football.

Some blamed the police,
some blamed the ground
and some blamed the fans themselves.
But most thought
it was just a terrible, terrible tragedy.

The whole country was stunned,
but in Liverpool itself
it seemed every family
had lost someone close.

They opened Anfield to the fans.
Thousands came in silence
and stood on the Kop,
crying quietly.
They tied the red scarves of Liverpool
to the railings in memory.
The whole of the Kop
was covered in red scarves.
They were called the flowers of Anfield.
Kenny Dalglish said,
'It was the most beautiful
and the saddest sight I have ever seen.'

The players moved among the fans,
talking to them,
trying to help.

Alan Hansen went to about 12 funerals.
He said,
'I'm not the best at these sort of things,
because I don't think I'm very strong.
They were getting worse and worse for me.
You start off thinking,
"By the time you go to five or six,
you'll get used to it,"
but they were getting worse
at the end for me.'

6 Liverpool Today

After Hillsborough,
something went out of Liverpool.
For years they did not win much
and their name was hated by many
because of Heysel.

All that changed in 2005,
in one of the greatest games ever.
It was the Champions League Final.
Liverpool were playing AC Milan.
Nobody gave Liverpool a chance.
They had scraped through the early stages
and were only in the Final
because of a lucky goal against Chelsea.
From the start Milan were on top.
It wasn't long before they were one up.
Then two.
Then three.
Three-nil to Milan at half-time!
They were sure they had won.

Everyone was sure they had won.
Everyone except Liverpool.
Steve Gerrard, the captain, inspired them.
They came out for the second half
a changed team.
They knocked Milan back with three goals in five
minutes and then held on until extra time.

Milan threw everything at them
but Liverpool still held on.
Now it was penalties!
And then the hero stepped forward –
Jerzy Dudek, the goalkeeper.
He had already made a miracle save in extra time
and now the pressure on him was huge.
He saved three penalties
and Liverpool won the Champions League!

Steven Gerrard, the Liverpool captain,
in the Champions League Final against Milan, 2005.

Everyone went wild.
Congratulations poured in –
from the Queen, from the Prime Minister
and from all over Europe.
When the team came back to Liverpool
nearly a million fans went to greet them.

This is the team that has walked on,
through the rain and wind,
and has always held its head up high.
Now 'the golden sky at the end of the storm'
is once again shining over Anfield.